HOW TO BE A
HAPPY
OLD MAN

a little guide
for grumpy
old men

George
Evans

Crombie Jardine
Publishing Limited
Office 2
3 Edgar Buildings
George Street
Bath
BA1 2FJ

www.crombiejardine.com

This edition was first published by
Crombie Jardine Publishing Limited in 2007

ISBN 978-1-906051-11-2

Written by George Evans

Typesetting and cover design
by Ben Ottridge

Printed and bound in China

CONTENTS

INTRODUCTION

Do you really want to be happy? Then forget about being sexy, important, wealthy, famous, athletic, popular... Manage without the harem, yacht, island, palace, Ferrari, wifelets... Just give it all up and be HAPPY!

Convinced that your happiness is the most important thing you've got, or ever want? Great! Join the HOM Club. Never mind about ruling the world, though I'm sure you will agree that you could do it better than the idiots in charge. Who cares about being youthful, athletic or handsome? We've been there, done that and got the scars to prove it.

Joking apart, there really are some simple ways to make your life much happier as you get older and that's what this little book is really all about.

Not worrying about yourself is part of it. Begin by not taking life too seriously. That means you don't have to worry about anyone else.

Y ou *do* need a HOW (Happy Old Woman). You please yourself but those with HOWs realise how important they can be. The key is in a song, 'I want to be happy but I can't be happy 'til I make you happy too'.

There are rules for keeping your HOW in good condition. If you can't turn them into standing jokes, you have problems.

Rule No. 1:

NEVER WIN AN ARGUMENT.
She's always right, especially when she's obviously not.

Rule No. 2:

IT'S ALWAYS YOUR FAULT.
That goes for lost handbags, global warming, etc.

Rule No. 3:

NEVER FORGET BIRTHDAYS,
ANNIVERSARIES ETC.
Penance can sometimes be
very expensive.

Invest time and trouble; your
HOW is worth it.

SERIOUSLY – don't take yourself too seriously. You are the only *you* in the whole wide world so there's no competition. You have to be the best there is.

If you stop worrying about that, there's nobody else to get into a sweat about. Be kind to the rest of the world; it's not their fault if they're not as good as you.

Friends are the people whose imperfections you are prepared to put up with. It's unreasonable to expect them to be perfect but they can, and usually do, contribute to your happiness, so keep them. Only your HOW is perfect. Remind her often.

Important people have their problems, the biggest of which is trying to look important. If they give you trouble, try laughing.

ENEMIES you can do without. Who needs enemies? You don't! It may be your Christian duty to forgive them but if you play your cards right you won't have any enemies to forgive. That's much better.

Life without enemies is so much easier, more comfortable and happier that it's hard to understand why anybody bothers with them.

If you don't do anyone harm and are generally cheerful and

friendly, most people won't want to be your enemy. If someone insists on treating you badly, here are a few suggestions:

DO THEM A FAVOUR

BE GENEROUS

LIKE THEM

LAUGH WITH THEM

WALK AWAY

OUTLIVE THEM (last resort)!

GRUMPY old men are going through a stage like babies and teenagers. Remember how it was? It's like train spotting, hero worship, hating girls, chasing girls, thinking you're important; things like that.

Perhaps you've been through it all. It's just part of life's rich pattern. They grow out of it eventually.

You must have friends who fit into this category. Don't blame them, it's part of human development. With patient help from you they will soon want to experience the next (and much more enjoyable) part of growing up: the Happy

Old Man syndrome. Teach them to be HOMs.

While you wait for light to dawn on them you can have fun leading them on to blame the weather on the Government. That's a good laugh.

HURRYING is for the young – it's not for you. There's a chap who gave up hurrying on VE Day, 8th May 1945, when the Germans stopped shooting at him. He said that when you've been comprehensively shot at by really well trained soldiers for nearly a year there is no further need to hurry when they've stopped.

Getting older is a good excuse for refusing to hurry. Take life gently. Chaps who hurry live shorter and less happy lives, so we don't want that. Let's just take our time. Remember the sexy song, 'An Englishman takes time'?

There's a new campaign for slow food and slow cities. Let's join it. The idea is that taking your time allows you to enjoy life more. That's a very important principle of the HOM movement.

HEALTH is, of course, very important. It's hard to be happy with a toothache or a pain in the back. Staying healthy is partly luck but there are things you can do to improve your lot.

Mother-in-law's dictum, 'Trust in the Lord and keep your

bowels open' is well worth obeying. So is 'An apple a day keeps the doctor away'. Sensible eating of varied meals and taking your time to digest them is the best advice. Most modern diets are written to persuade daft people to read the books or buy the food. If your HOW is a good cook, you're very fortunate;

remember to tell her so – frequently. Otherwise, start learning.

Exercise is good if it's regular and gentle. Don't compete with others; just do what you enjoy. All competitive games are unhealthy. Most, if not all, top athletes are injured at some stage, often more than once. Don't hurt yourself.

HABITS can be very good for you. Most of us have regular habits, like getting up at a set time, brewing tea or taking the dog for a walk. Think about the habits that make up your day. Don't write them all down; it would take too long. Habits save us the bother of thinking out each move. Hurrah for good habits!

Sometimes we can get into bad habits, or even time-wasting ones. These need thinking about, analysing and maybe changing.

Take, for instance, shaving. If that takes too long or is a great trouble, consider the alternatives. You could grow a beard (with your HOW's permission) or simply change your system – different razor, soap, gel, time, place or whatever.

Or you may find supper is making you stay awake when you'd rather be asleep.

HEADOLOGY is about what goes on in your head. That's where you feel things and happiness is a state of mind. Is it possible to improve your Happiness Quotient by thinking the right thoughts? You bet it is, though it's not easy.

First you need time to think and a quiet, comfortable place where you won't be disturbed. A good start is to count your blessings. You're still here, so that's good. There are plenty of things about you that are pleasing. Count them all; tick them on paper when you've run out of fingers and toes.

HAVE fun! It's very important to your happiness. There are plenty of things in this world to laugh about, so make sure you recognise them.

Young people – and by that I mean anyone who still has to work for a living – are great fun. Be kind to them; they're paying into the pension fund, so you have something to be grateful for.

Small children can be good fun – for a short time. Try not to let them exhaust you and do give them back before they become a handful.

Teenagers can be exciting to know. Don't mind if they know

much less than they think they do; it's par for the course. Try listening to them; nobody else does and some good ideas will come out. They'll try your patience of course; remember you were like that once.

FAMILIES can be most enjoyable or not, as the case may be. George Burns, the American comedian, used to say that happiness is a large, loving family – in another town.

Families are a Good Thing but you can have enough of a Good Thing. There are

HOMs who are very fond of their grandchildren but can't remember the names of all of them. Perhaps that's an ideal position if you have been putting your DNA around rather a lot.

Responsibility is all very well – we're responsible for our own children, of course, but they in turn are responsible for theirs.

It helps if you develop a reputation for incompetence, especially an inability to do the things you hate doing.

HOBBIES are what you do for fun. Very often they represent the job you would like to be paid for but never found anyone willing to pay you to do.

Some people who would have loved to have been writers take up writing as a hobby after retiring because they don't feel the pressure of having to earn a living any longer. So instead of writing to please an editor or publisher they can write whatever and whenever they wish.

There's a danger of being obsessed with the equipment though. Photographers, for instance, tend to read photo magazines without realising that these magazines are aimed at promoting their advertisers who are trying to sell you the gear and you don't need it all.

But you do need something to do.

YOUR memories are an essential part of you. To achieve a sort of everlasting life you can write down your memories so they will live after you.

Who is interested? Your family and friends first, but also future historians. There are never enough accounts of day-to-day life in any historical period. Historians drool over the personal stories of long gone people.

Have your story published if you can but don't expect a huge advance from a big publisher; that might be nice if it happened but it rarely does. There are local organisations like historic societies, civic societies and so on. If there are none of these in your town, then give copies to the library, where they will be available to researchers forever.

C OLLECTIONS of photographs are of enormous help to historians, both local and national. It is difficult to find pictures of everyday life during the last World War for instance, partly because films were hard to get and also because, as in so many times, nobody thought of recording the ordinary details of life.

Things and habits go out of fashion and it seems nobody is

interested in them for a while.
Then suddenly they become
history and who can recall
them?

Here are a few examples
– wireless aerials, coal fires,
typewriters, steam trains,
punishment canes, washing
dollies, blue whitener, hobnailed
boots and gramophones.

What will we see as historic artefacts in the future? Motor cars? Laptops? Mobiles? Power stations? Snap them and make a record.

MONEY must not be one of your problems. The essential is to live within your means. The average British pensioner has a greater income than most third world villages. It's all a matter of balance. Provided you don't have too many expensive habits, like a bottle of scotch a day or your HOW needs a lot of retail therapy, all should be well.

Remember: money itself isn't the root of all evil, it's the

love of money; and you gave up the idea of being rich to concentrate on your happiness. Any expenditure to impress the neighbours should not be necessary.

What is important about you isn't what you own; it's what you are and what you do. Don't be impressed by other people's possessions either; possessions don't make better people.

BEING useful is very satisfying; it makes you feel better; it gives you a reason for living. Of course your HOW will need a lot of TLC; that will keep you quite busy.

Lots of older folk take up voluntary jobs and enjoy doing them very much. Some of these are organised by hospitals, clubs and charities but many are far less formal, like helping friends, family and neighbours.

If, when doing your voluntary job, you feel you're not

appreciated, you can always say so. It's not like at work when you depend on the pay; now you have the option of just stopping. But do say as politely as possible whenever you feel like giving up rather than letting resentment build up.

Make sure you enjoy the work.

WORKING for money is what we all did. After going to work every day for forty years or so it's a big change to have to wonder what to do every morning.

To begin with, retired life seems all one long holiday, but without the job to come back to, the holidays can get a bit boring. There's a need to have a routine or there's nothing to have a holiday from.

As we get older things take longer to do and life fills with day-to-day things. Breakfast can take a couple of hours and suddenly it's time for coffee. That takes at least an hour, after which it's lunch time, then there's a nap – see how boring it gets?

We need regular and irregular breaks when there are other things to do. Try to balance routine and change. Occasional revolutions might help.

WORK tends to expand to fill the time available. One of the reasons we are all so busy in retirement is that we do things far more slowly.

It's best to ration yourself to one excitement a day whenever possible. To have a day without any excitement at all can be boring but you can have too much of a Good Thing and tire yourself out, resulting in a lack of enjoyment.

Some stimulation is needed, though it doesn't have to come from outside. Sit and wonder what to do next. A well-known local preacher used to ask his driver, 'What shall we give 'em today? Shall we give 'em bloody hellfire?'

Think – is it going to be fun? Will it be a good laugh?

GARDENING is very popular but it's also seasonable and even in the best seasons it depends on the weather.

There's a saying that you're nearer your death in the garden than anywhere else on Earth. There's some truth in that, for so many ancients have accidents, falling out of trees they should have known better than to climb.

All this shouldn't stop you doing what you enjoy; just be careful.

If you need an excuse for *not* gardening, think of this: if you do nothing and neglect your garden for fifty years it'll probably be designated as an Area of Outstanding Natural Beauty; The Man Upstairs is a better gardener than anyone on the telly; Nature rules OK.

In non-gardening weather all keen gardeners have to find

themselves something else to do. Well, there's the thrill of cleaning and oiling tools, tidying up the shed and making compost.

Another idea, for 'impossible' days is to plan things for next year or when you can get out there again. Start with what you've got – as it is now – and then wonder about it. What do you want to *do* in your garden? Is it just to look at, to impress the neighbours, or is it something more dynamic?

If you have youngsters coming round there's got to be a play space and a hidyhole. Perhaps a pond is needed? Your HOW will probably want somewhere to have a picnic. You might want to read a good book. Don't make a rod for your own back. If it's not fun, don't do it.

SLEEP is very good medicine. Some of us could sleep for Britain if they had it in the Olympics. By all means spend a warm summer afternoon dozing in the garden. Why ever not? Just remember to wear a hat, especially if you've a bald patch or involuntary tonsure.

Don't let them tell you that you are lazy; laugh that one off. Now you can sleep when you feel like it, rather than when convention or someone else says you may. It has been said that, 'Early risers are conceited in the morning and tired in the afternoon.' But if you're naturally an early bird, don't let that put you off getting up early and having a nap after lunch – and tea – and any other time you like.

If you need pills to sleep it's probably because you picked the wrong time.

MEDICINES should be avoided unless absolutely necessary. Doctors, with the best will in the world, tend to give out too many pills. Most will admit it.

Often what is needed is a change of habits or lifestyle but they can't prescribe that on the NHS. If you break a couple of floating ribs they'll only give you pain killers. The ribs will cure themselves if you're healthy and sensible. The hurt goes off with gentle exercise and time.

Some say that aspirins, Germolene and alcohol are the only medicines you need.

An old mumming play says, 'I can cure a magpie of the

toothache.' 'How do you do that?' 'Cut his head off.'

Pills all have side effects, which don't affect people who don't take them. Just wonder at that.

TIREDNESS can be a problem. Is it really caused by lack of sleep or just trapped wind? That has much the same effect on your mind – which is where you feel everything.

Wind – up and down – can be an 'old folks' problem. Why are we called 'old farts?' Does it really matter? No.

TIME-RICH is what we are supposed to be and there's a lot of truth in that. We do have more time but some of this is used up doing the usual things more slowly. We also have friends who think that now we've retired there's plenty of time to do what they want us to do.

A good rule of thumb? If it's going to be fun, do it; otherwise, don't!

If you don't want to do something, just say 'No' rather than half commit yourself with a 'I'll have a think about it'.

We do have more time to think things over, with the result

that we tend to make fewer mistakes. Hurrying is for the young. It's a safe bet that anyone much younger than yourself is in a bigger hurry. Let them get on with it.

BE selfish – do good for your own sake. When you do someone a favour it makes you feel good. Every time you do something you know is right it makes you happy. Hating others, even when you might think there's a good reason, makes you miserable yourself.

All the best religions have much the same moral code and most agnostics and atheists agree with it. Behaving well, doing good to others, leading an honest, decent life… these are the right ways to live, whatever you believe.

Forgiving your neighbour his faults is not only easier

than beating him up or less expensive than taking him to law, it's actually more likely to make you happy. Helping out other people is very pleasant and gives you a warm glow. Truthfulness is much easier on the memory.

RELIGION is a problem for some people and a great help to others. It really depends what you mean by 'religion'. Those who believe in a bad-tempered, angry God who wants them to hate all His enemies will find it difficult to live in the modern world and even more difficult to be happy.

Does it really matter what you believe? Or is it more important how you behave? Some folks seem to think they were put on Earth to keep the population down by killing in the name of God. They don't seem happy people. Some religions expect their adherents to believe all sorts of apparently unlikely things that don't make much sense. But if that gives them a cosy feeling and encourages them to be happy and treat the rest of us well, why criticise?

MANY churches or other religious groups function as social communities, where people meet regularly in a friendly atmosphere. They are a great help to lonely souls and a pleasure to the rest when they are run well.

It is a great comfort to belong to some of the best, though there are often individuals who strain everyone's tolerance for their loquaciousness and loud voices or their moaning or pomposity. Often these are signs of low self-esteem covered up by trying too hard to compensate.

Do you ever wonder what percentage of the average congregation really does believe the creed of their church? Some, perhaps most, simply don't worry about such things. The routines, ceremonies and especially the atmosphere, are often a good reason for joining.

BELIEF in Easter Bunnies, Valhalla or Holy Rocks are all fine and don't disturb anyone's happiness if they make their adherents feel warm and comfortable.

But if any belief encourages
people to murder in the name
of a merciful, compassionate
God, then there's a good
reason to stay away from it.

Most of the world's great
religions have had leaders
at some time who have
encouraged their followers to
be paranoid and murderous.

It's a great wonder to see how the words of good, kind prophets have been twisted to hate.

HOMs know much better than that. We are engaged in the pursuit of happiness and we are not going any other way. As Ken Dodd sang, 'I thank the Lord that I am blessed with more than my share of happiness'.

IRRITATIONS should be avoided. If you irritate an oyster you get pearls but irritate a drunk and you might well have a bloody nose. Whatever you do, don't irritate your HOW. That is most certainly not the way to a happy old age.

So what if others irritate you? The short answer is, 'Don't let them.' Cultivate such an aura of tranquillity that nothing bothers you much. It's back to patience again. Remember the old pseudo-Latin tag, *Noli illigitimus carborundum*, which translates as, 'Don't let the b******s grind you down.' Laughter is always worth trying.

If someone else's odd habits annoy you, what are you going to do? Change them if you can do it gently, learn to live with them or, if it gets altogether too much, walk away. Just don't worry about it – or anything else.

QUIRKS are everybody's right: they are what make us human. We are all entitled to a quirk or two provided they aren't too annoying.

There should be a Society for the Preservation of Quirks. Actually, there are quite a few such bodies if you think about it; dozens of them, all beavering away with monthly meetings, exhibitions, museums, concerts, magazines, websites and handbooks.

Think of a few – the bagpipe museum, fox-hunting, modern art, skiffle, dead languages and pipe smoking all have adherents and why ever not?

Quirks are great fun – some of them anyway – and, provided they do no harm, let's encourage them.

BLAME is an idea that gets in the way of happiness. Too many people worry about who is to blame for everything that goes wrong and most of the time it doesn't really matter who's fault anything is.

The important thing is what are you going to do about it?

In the late 1930s and early 1940s young men all over the world joined their nation's armed forces to defend their homelands. Those who survived wished they hadn't joined up. All sorts of people and events have been blamed for the last World War which, like all wars, was very stupid.

It no longer matters (if it ever did) who's fault it was. What matters is learning how not to make the same terrible mistakes again.

When will they ever learn?

HEROES should be avoided – they lead you into trouble. That's the opinion of most soldiers who have been shot at. In fact the British and German infantry in the last World War agreed that the words 'hero' and 'idiot' are synonyms. Ordinary German conscripts used to call the SS heroes as an insult.

Anyway, far too many people nowadays are called heroes for scoring goals or acting in films. The word has degenerated like many others. It's fine to praise brave folks who have successfully rescued someone from peril or done some other meritorious act with no gain to themselves, but to call overpaid performers heroes brings the word into disrepute.

Forget heroism, aim for happiness. Happy people last longer.

HONOURS should be looked at askance. Perhaps it's fair to suggest that the pursuit of honours should be avoided like the plague.

Governments tend to hand out their gongs to those who have been already well paid for the work they did. The other way of achieving an honour is to help a political party by getting their candidate elected or by chairing committees. Whilst some recipients do really earn their honours, many worthy contenders go without.

Promotion to the House of Lords by doing a political favour has been going on for several centuries. Many great noble families began when a pretty daughter warmed the king's bed.

Never mind chasing honours; we're HOMs and all we want is long term happiness.

CELEBRITY is a word in vogue at the moment. What exactly is a celebrity? What does the word mean? The best definition so far is, 'Someone who is famous for being well known'.

Often they occupy our TV screens and we wonder what they do for a living. Usually it seems to be to shout incomprehensible words into a microphone or play a bit part in a film. All that's needed is a good agent.

One most celebrated king of England was Richard the Lion Heart. He was probably the worst king we ever had, spending a fortune on a stupid war and having to be rescued at great cost. But his minstrel, Blondin, was a great agent.

No thanks; we HOMs don't want to be celebrities – just happy.

WEALTH is dangled before us all the time. Many people – too many – seem to judge the importance and worthiness of the rest of us by our bank balances. Or, perhaps more likely, by the amount of money we flash around, which is not at all the same thing.

This is nothing new either. Think about the stately homes dotted around the country; the sort now owned by the National Trust. All these were built by the rich to impress the credulous natives. The reason the Trust now owns them is often that the family went broke.

It has been said that, 'Money may not bring happiness but it helps you to be miserable in comfort.'

Misery is misery, no matter how comfortable it may be. We don't want to be miserable. What do we want? Happy old age!

STARS seem to be all over the place; film stars, soccer stars, TV stars, sports stars, and so on, surrounded by worshipful 'fans' who cheer, scream and try to grab bits of them. This has been going on for thousands of years since Roman triumphs. It gives the 'stars' delusions of grandeur for a while.

All too often these poor people, when the adulation and their prowess are exhausted, find themselves in most unhappy circumstances. Their supporters have found other idols or just grown up; their money has been taken by tricksters or taxmen and they are living in misery.

Stardom is not for HOMs. It might be nice for a time but unless you pick just the right time to opt out and return to Earth, being a star can easily become a road to disaster. Let's just be happy.

NAUGHTY things are often fun. Do you think happiness can be enhanced by occasionally doing something just a little bit naughty?

Perhaps it depends on whether anyone else is hurt by our naughtiness. We wouldn't like that, even though we all know people who are asking to be made fun of.

The key question when playing a joke on someone is whether they think it's funny. Not just that they laugh (they may be secretly seething) but if they really enjoy the joke.

The safest quips are against yourself. To get out of doing something you really hate it's often a good ploy to describe yourself as an incompetent idiot. Just hope your friends don't take that too seriously.

WRINKLY power seems a very good idea. If only the world were run by someone with our experience of life, our understanding and knowledge it would surely be a much better place. The trouble is that it isn't and is never likely to be. Countries led by old chaps tend to be stuck in their ancient ways and the man in charge spends most of his energy remaining in office.

All we can usefully do is tolerate the situation we are in and just occasionally offer a bit of advice in a friendly way. Or laugh at it.

You can sometimes be constructive when you persuade some energetic young chap that he thought of your idea himself and gets it done. This amounts to influence without power. Then, if it goes wrong, it's not your fault.

ACHES and pains are par for the course. As we get older we seem to accumulate the odd problem now and then and gradually they add up.

Also there are the genetically programmed medical matters like arthritis and a bald head. These may well leave you alone for many years until they finally catch up.

'Thanks for the bald head, Grandad.'

Some of our disadvantages we may take to the doctor for some medicine to alleviate them. The trouble with this is that all his pills are potentially poisonous and have 'side effects'.

It's best, often, to just learn to live with whatever ails us, especially if the alternative is worse. As they say...

WHAT CAN'T BE CURED MUST BE ENDURED.

G ROWING up is something we are all supposed to do. But what do you call a completely grown-up person?

Young children are not expected to behave in a responsible way and we have to be responsible for them. Put a catch on the front gate and you have until the child learns how to open it to teach them not to run out on the road.

Teenagers are too often told to 'act their age' when that's just what they are doing.

As we mature we are all expected to become more

responsible for everything and to think, 'I am a responsible man; if something's wrong I am responsible.' But a bit of us never wanted to grow up and as we age that part struggles to the surface again.

A completely grown-up human being is called a *woman*. Ask your HOW.

KINDNESS is well worthwhile for selfish reasons; because it makes you feel good. That includes, perhaps especially, the kind things you do without expecting – or getting – any thanks for them.

Of course it's nice to be thanked for our Good Deeds

and more often than not the recipient will be well enough brought-up to say, 'Thank you'.

When others don't thank us there's no point in worrying about it or being resentful. That won't make us happy – in fact just the opposite – so we don't bother with it.

Beware of doing what you think is a kind act but turns out just the opposite. Think it through before you act. Remember the story of the Boy Scout who was beaten up by an old lady who didn't want to cross the road.

WORRYING is not good for you – so don't do it. That's much easier said than done but it's worthwhile trying, even though it needs a little thought and concentration. First wonder about what it is that worries you. Then resolve to do something about it. Then do it.

Are you worrying about something in your past? Making mistakes is quite normal; you're only human. The man who never made a mistake never made anything.

Worriers and happy people are not the same breed. Your worries have to be disposed of, so get on and do it. Whatever it is that troubles you either put it right or forget it.

Pack up your troubles in your old kit bag and smile, smile, smile.

S MILING, even when there's not a lot to smile at, gets you by in life far more happily than miserable folks. Spread a few happy grins around the world and do a favour to yourself and everyone you meet.

When you don't particularly feel like smiling, that's the time to work hardest at it.

We all know people who are racked with pain, yet seem to carry round with them a kind of cheerful euphoria. They spread an aura of goodwill, accepting their fate and making the most of what they've got.

Practise smiling every day. Shaving time is often the most convenient moment. Put a bit of energy into it. Throw yourself into a great big cheesy grin; the mirror will tell you if you have it right; and mean it. Do it *now*. Good.

SELF-ESTEEM is worth a lot. Others won't think much of you if you don't rate yourself. Remember you are the finest possible you because you're the only one.

Count your blessings. Make a list of the things you can do, what you have done, who you are and what you've got.

George Burns used to wander onto the stage when he was over ninety and say, 'I'm glad to be here. At my age, I'm glad to be anywhere.' 'All is for the best in the best of worlds,' said Candide, and since there is only the one world, then this must be the best! That may be cock-eyed optimism but it beats pessimism any day.

Building your own opinion of yourself is an exercise worth a lot of effort.

PHILOSOPHY. What is that exactly? My dictionary says it's seeking wisdom or knowledge, especially that which deals with ultimate reality.

Perhaps that's what we have been doing for many years, like the chap who didn't know he was talking prose.

Textbooks on philosophy, seem a different matter, however. They appear to consist of navel-gazing, stealing ideas from other philosophers, academic bitchiness and arguments about irrelevant ideas. Who cares how many angels can dance on the head of a pin?

But we all need a basic philosophy of life, an idea of what is the ultimate reality. Perhaps it's best to work it out for ourselves, even if it makes no more sense than the philosophers.

TRANQUILITY is a lovely thought. How good it is when life becomes simple, easy, peaceful and quiet.

Some people achieve tranquility, or at least something like it, regularly by meditation, prayer, or simply being on their own doing nothing in particular.

Chanting old, well-remembered prayers or mantras can induce a calm state of mind. So can emptying your mind and thinking of nothing.

Do we spend too much of our time bothering about silly little day-to-day things? Surely we do. It has to be worth the effort to shovel the clutter to one side for a few moments to gain a tranquil state now and then.

Yoga and Quakerism have suggestions to make which work for their adherents.

HEAVEN and Hell – in this world at least – exist in our own heads. They are just states of mind that can be very real.

'The Kingdom of Heaven is within you,' said the Man from Nazareth, and as usual he was right. He could also have said the same for Hell.   Perhaps that's what this little book is really all about – wrapping your mind around the idea of happiness and treating that as a main aim in life.

Our way of thinking is that at least one important aim in life is to be happy. That's very like saying we want to be in Heaven while we're still on Earth. And why not? It has to be worth a try anyway.

So let's try to live, behave and think in ways that will make us – and our HOWs – happy for the rest of our days. After that – who knows?

SPACE and time are important for you and your HOW. You both need to be able to be yourselves as individuals as well as part of the team of two. It just doesn't make sense to be in each other's pockets all the time.

Why can't a woman be more like a man? For perfectly good biological reasons – that's why. Wouldn't it be a terribly dull world if we were all the same? Of course that makes for differences but variety is the spice of life.

Try to forgive her when she's right as well as when she's

wrong. Bottling up differences can have worse consequences than a shouting match, so be as open as you can.

There's only one sensible way to treat a woman you have chosen to spend your life with – just simply love her with everything you've got.

LOVE is for giving away. You give it to your HOW and to your family. It's not just a one-off gift; it needs to be constantly repeated, often several times a day. The more you give away the more you have, even when there seems no response.

Giving is good for you. Happiness is inside you and can spread a warm glow around. All the world loves a lover.

True love grows as the years go by. Some of this may be due to the fact that you had all the arguments in your youth and they have been settled many years ago. When they recur it's easier to resolve them.

The more love you give away, the more you have left. That may not make sense mathematically, but it's a fact.

FRIENDSHIP is what you give to the rest of the world. 'A stranger is a friend you've not yet met,' as they say.

There are no totally bad people on Earth – or at least you never meet one. All we know about super-villains like Hitler, Stalin or Mao is what we've been told by reporters who never met them either. When you get to know even the most obnoxious people it's possible to find extenuating circumstances.

Sometimes, of course, it isn't easy to treat others as friends, especially when they are really annoying you. But many soldiers, when they've stopped trying to kill each other, are happy to shake hands. If they can do that, surely we can all befriend anyone else. It's worth the effort.

Befriend your enemies and they'll change.

HONESTY, truth and openness are all qualities well worth cultivating for your own pursuit of happiness. They may not make you rich, but then you can't have it all. We were going to give up trying to be affluent and concentrate on being happy...

The English (or perhaps it was the British) used to be famous for 'fair play'. That was before it became more fashionable to win at all costs. Children accepted punishment for sins they really had committed and parents didn't send for a lawyer.

Honesty and truth save you from cheating and telling lies, so they're easier on the memory. Openness saves the trouble of hiding things away. 'Tell the truth and shame the Devil' is a good maxim.

ACCEPTING who we are and what we are can be a great relief. Like everybody else, we're going to die some time and what's the point of pretending otherwise? As we get older we should prepare for that, though it's not easy to come to terms with.

We also become weaker in body and mind, though not so quickly if we exercise both of them.

Ambitions tend to fly away. We have either realised most of them or given up. We're not going to be Olympic Champions at anything. But it might be good to be the oldest chap to do something, like walk up a favourite hill, swim a mile or run a marathon.

Let's just accept ourselves as the individuals we are – 'warts and all' as Oliver Cromwell said. No illusions; we are just ourselves.

WARNING:

This book was written by a retired teacher, so there will now be revision, followed by the final examination.

Revision:

1. Spend a lot of time on your HOW.
2. Befriend everyone you meet.
3. Be happy for the rest of your life.

Final examination:

Chief examiner – St Peter.
Place of exam – Golden Gates.
Syllabus – Your life history.

Good luck!

The World's Funniest Laws

JAMES ALEXANDER

In Arizona you can go to prison for 25 years for cutting down a cactus!

Do not say "oh boy" in Jonesborough, Georgia. It's illegal!

On Sundays in Florida, widows must not go parachuting!

It is against the law to take a lion to the cinema in Baltimore!

ISBN 978-1-905102-10-5, £4.99, pb

The World's Funniest Proverbs

JAMES ALEXANDER

Beauty is in the eye of the beer holder

Don't take life too seriously - it's not permanent

Multi-tasking: the art of screwing up everything all at once

Never marry for money; you will borrow cheaper

ISBN 978-1-906051-07-5, £5.99, hb

The World's Funniest Puns

Archaeologist: A man whose career lies in ruins.

What's the definition of a will? A dead giveaway.

Did you hear about the butcher who backed into a meat grinder? He got a little behind in his work.

JAMES ALEXANDER

ISBN 978-1-905102-33-2, £4.99, pb

All Crombie Jardine books are
available from high street bookshops,
Littlehampton Book Services,
www.amazon.co.uk and Bookpost
(P.O. Box 29, Douglas, Isle of Man, IM99 1BQ
email: bookpost@enterprise.net
www.bookpost.co.uk
tel: 01624 677237
p & p free within the UK).

www.crombiejardine.com

www.crombiejardine.com